US ARMED FORCES

JOIN THE
NAVY

By P. P. Mitchell

Gareth Stevens
PUBLISHING

HOT TOPICS

T0018306

Please visit our website, www.garethstevens.com. For a free color catalog of all our high-quality books, call toll free 1-800-542-2595 or fax 1-877-542-2596.

Library of Congress Cataloging-in-Publication Data

Names: Mitchell, P. P., author.
Title: Join the Navy / P.P. Mitchell.
Description: New York : Gareth Stevens Publishing, 2018. | Series: US Armed
  Forces | Includes index.
Identifiers: LCCN 2017001360| ISBN 9781538205488 (pbk. book) | ISBN
  9781538205495 (6 pack) | ISBN 9781538205501 (library bound book)
Subjects: LCSH: United States. Navy--Juvenile literature. | United States.
  Navy--Vocational guidance--Juvenile literature.
Classification: LCC VB259 .M57 2018 | DDC 359.0023/73--dc23
LC record available at https://lccn.loc.gov/2017001360

Published in 2018 by
Gareth Stevens Publishing
111 East 14th Street, Suite 349
New York, NY 10003

Copyright © 2018 Gareth Stevens Publishing

Designer: Bethany Perl
Editor: Joan Stoltman

Photo credits: Cover, 1-32 (camouflage) Casper1774 Studio/Shutterstock.com; cover, pp. 1-32 (grunge effect) iulias/Shutterstock.com; cover, pp. 1-32 (rounded text box) foxie/ Shutterstock.com; cover, pp. 1-31 (border) jumpingsack/Shutterstock.com; pp. 2-32 (text box) Olga_C/Shutterstock.com; p. 5 Leonard Zhukovsky/Shutterstock.com; pp. 5-29 (dog tag) Feng Yu/Shutterstock.com; photos courtesy of US Navy: cover, p. 1 by Mass Communication Specialist 2nd Class Jared King, p. 5, by Steven L. Shepard, Presidio of Monterey Public Affairs, p. 7 by Mass Communication Specialist 2nd Class John Herman, p. 9 by Mass Communication Specialist 2nd Class Antonio P. Turretto, p. 13 by Mass Communication Specialist Seaman Zach Sleeper, p. 15 by Cpl. Samantha K. Braun, p. 17 by Mass Communication Specialist 3rd Class Danny Kelley, p. 27 by Mass Communication Specialist Seaman David Flewllyn, p. 29 by Tim Jensen, p. 30 (Service Uniform) by Mass Communication Specialist 2nd Class Ryan J. Batchelder, p. 30 (Service Dress Blues) Mass Communication Specialist 1st Class Greg Johnson; p. 11, 29 (American Flag) Nataliia K/Shutterstock.com; p. 19 MILpicturesby Tom Weber/The Image Bank/ Getty Images; p. 21 Official U.S. Navy Page/Wikipedia.org; p. 23 YASUYOSHI CHIBA/Staff/ AFP/Getty Images; p. 25 Steve Kaufman/Corbis Documentary/Getty Images; p. 30 (Working Uniform) U.S.Navy/Handout/Getty Image News/Getty Images.

Printed in China

CPSIA compliance information: Batch #CS17GS: For further information contact Gareth Stevens, New York, New York at 1-800-542-2595.

CONTENTS

ALL ABOUT THE NAVY!

Do you want to travel the world and learn how other people live while serving the United States? The US Navy has proudly served and bravely led all over the world since 1775!

DID YOU KNOW?

Men and women alike are called sailors in the navy! And since 2016, women can have any job in the navy.

From pulling people out of dangerous conditions to fighting during a war, the navy's there. Over 320,000 sailors are stationed all over the world. This allows the navy to get there quickly when called with the tools they need.

DID YOU KNOW?

Since 50 percent of all people live near a coast, the navy is a very important part of the armed forces and is often called on.

You'll need to know all about ships in the navy. Some ships are huge, like an aircraft carrier. Other ships are small, like coastal patrol ships. The navy also uses submarines, which quietly work underwater.

DID YOU KNOW?
The navy has over 100 ships and 3,700 aircraft—including airplanes and helicopters—in operation right now!

HOW CAN I JOIN?

There are two paths to joining the navy: sign up, or enlist, as a sailor or become an officer. To enlist, speak to a **recruiter** once you're 18 and have finished high school. After passing some tests, you're off to boot camp for training!

NAVY RANKS

OFFICERS

FLEET ADMIRAL

ADMIRAL

VICE ADMIRAL

REAR ADMIRAL UPPER
      HALF

REAR ADMIRAL LOWER
      HALF

CAPTAIN

COMMANDER

LIEUTENANT COMMANDER

LIEUTENANT

LIEUTENANT, JUNIOR
      GRADE

ENSIGN

ENLISTED

MASTER CHIEF PETTY
      OFFICER OF THE NAVY

MASTER CHIEF PETTY
      OFFICER

SENIOR CHIEF PETTY
      OFFICER

CHIEF PETTY OFFICER

PETTY OFFICER FIRST CLASS

PETTY OFFICER SECOND
      CLASS

PETTY OFFICER THIRD
      CLASS SEAMAN

SEAMAN APPRENTICE

SEAMAN RECRUIT

DID YOU KNOW?

A rank is a title that shows your responsibility, or duty, in the armed forces. Enlisted sailors and officers are ranked separately.

To become an officer, you must first finish school at a 4-year college with good grades. After college, you'll train at officer **candidate** school. If you've gone to school to become a doctor, **nuclear engineer**, nurse, or pilot, you'll train at officer **development** school.

DID YOU KNOW?

Enlisted sailors can become officers by completing additional training in naval history, traditions, order, and leadership.

You can also become an officer
by going to the Naval Academy
in Annapolis, Maryland.
You'll need great grades
and community service and
leadership experience. You can
also be in the Naval Reserve
Officer Training Corps
program while taking classes
at over 160 colleges.

DID YOU KNOW?
The Naval Academy has many famous former students, including 19 American **ambassadors**, 24 members of Congress, five state governors, 53 astronauts, and one president, Jimmy Carter!

JOBS IN THE NAVY

There are hundreds of different jobs you can have in the navy. You can break spy codes, fix a submarine, order a ship's supplies, invent weapons, and much more. Navy divers save, build, repair, search, and more—all underwater!

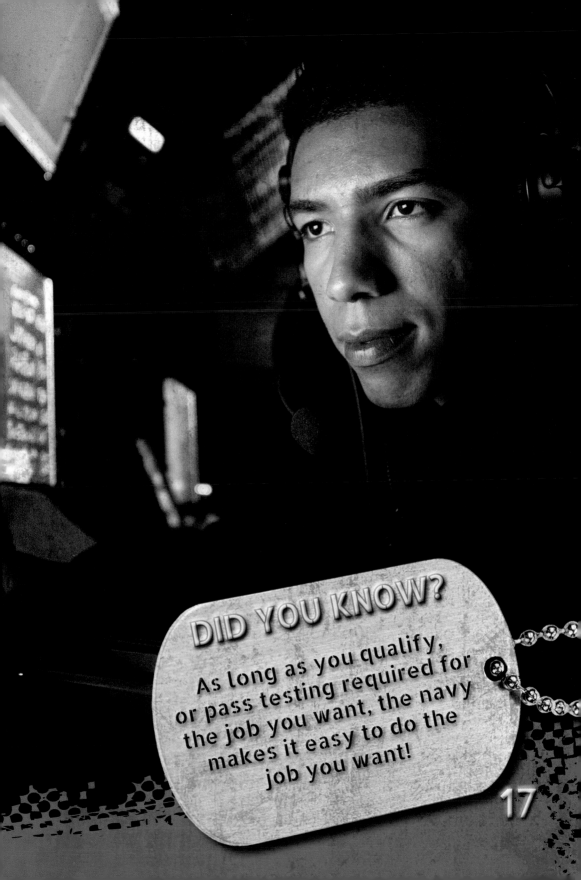

DID YOU KNOW?

As long as you qualify, or pass testing required for the job you want, the navy makes it easy to do the job you want!

17

NAVY SEALs

Navy SEALs are some of the best-trained fighters in the world. SEALs go on **missions** others can't do. They get quick results, all due to their training, which is possibly the toughest military training out there!

DID YOU KNOW?

"SEAL" stands for "sea, air, and land," because Navy SEALs are trained for missions in all three!

WHAT'S LIFE LIKE IN THE NAVY?

There are more than 100 navy bases and ports around the world! Bases are like towns, with grocery stores, movie theaters, gyms, hospitals, and libraries. If stationed, or sent to work, at a base, you'll live and work near a coast.

20

DID YOU KNOW?

There are around 265,000 enlisted sailors, and over 54,000 officers serving in the navy!

Once part of the navy, you'll spend time at sea living on a ship! Sailors are commonly appointed to a ship for 3 years, but you'll often be docked at a port and not at sea. Time at sea depends on missions and the ship you're on.

23

Living on a submarine is very different from how you live now. There isn't a lot of space, and getting in touch with family and friends is hard. But you'll live inside an awesome machine with the latest spy **technology**!

DID YOU KNOW?

Sailors are able to get mail and packages whenever they're in port.

To work on a submarine, you'll pass tests and go through a year of training. Sailors must be able to work with technology, fight fires, control flooding, and be okay living in a cramped space and not speaking to loved ones.

DID YOU KNOW?

The navy has over 70 submarines total. Only 6 percent of sailors serve on submarines.

HOW CAN I GET READY NOW?

The navy recommends you get a head start on your training through daily exercise, like walking, jogging, swimming, biking, and other exercises or being on a sports team. Work to be a leader at school and in your community, too!

THE SAILOR'S CREED

I AM A UNITED STATES SAILOR. I WILL SUPPORT AND DEFEND THE CONSTITUTION OF THE UNITED STATES OF AMERICA AND I WILL OBEY THE ORDERS OF THOSE APPOINTED OVER ME. I REPRESENT THE FIGHTING SPIRIT OF THE NAVY AND THOSE WHO HAVE GONE BEFORE ME TO DEFEND FREEDOM AND DEMOCRACY AROUND THE WORLD. I PROUDLY SERVE MY COUNTRY'S NAVY COMBAT TEAM WITH HONOR, COURAGE AND COMMITMENT. I AM COMMITTED TO EXCELLENCE AND THE FAIR TREATMENT OF ALL.

DID YOU KNOW?

Get ready now by practicing the words of "The Sailor's Creed."

NAVY UNIFORMS

WORKING
UNIFORM

SERVICE
UNIFORM

SERVICE
DRESS
BLUES

FOR MORE INFORMATION

Books

Boothroyd, Jennifer. *Inside the US Navy*. Minneapolis, MN: Lerner Publications, 2017.

Bozzo, Linda. *U.S. Navy*. Mankato, MN: Amicus High Interest, 2014.

Gordon, Nick. *Navy SEALs*. Minneapolis, MN: Bellwether Media, 2013.

Websites

Naval Heritage

history.navy.mil/browse-by-topic/heritage.html

Read more about the history of the navy!

Navy Careers & Jobs

navy.com/navy/careers.html

Explore all the different kinds of jobs you can have in the navy!

Submarine Facts for Kids

sciencekids.co.nz/sciencefacts/vehicles/submarines.html

Read all about these awesome underwater ships.

GLOSSARY

ambassador: someone sent by one group or country to speak for it in different places

candidate: a person who is being considered for a job, position or award

development: the act of growing and changing

mission: a task or job a group must perform

nuclear engineer: a person trained to use science and math to work with nuclear power, a form of energy that's used to power submarines

recruiter: the person in a community who helps people enlist in the armed forces

technology: the way people do something using tools and the tools that they use

INDEX